What Lives on a Sandy Beach?

by Catherine Halversen
illustrated by Barbara Schaffer

Published and Distributed by
Delta Education
...because children learn by doing.®
A member of School Specialty Science

Published and Distributed by

These materials are based upon work partially supported by the National Science Foundation under grant number ESI-0242733. The Federal Government has certain rights in this material. Any opinions, findings, and conclusions or recommendations expressed in this material are those of the author(s) and do not necessarily reflect the views of the National Science Foundation.

Developed at Lawrence Hall of Science and the Graduate School of Education at the University of California at Berkeley

Seeds of Science/Roots of Reading™ is a collaboration of a science team led by Jacqueline Barber and a literacy team led by P. David Pearson and Gina Cervetti.

Delta Education LLC
PO Box 3000
Nashua, NH 03061
1-800-258-1302
www.deltaeducation.com

What Lives on a Sandy Beach?
594-0005
ISBN-10: 1-59821-479-9
ISBN-13: 978-1-59821-479-6
1 2 3 4 5 6 7 8 9 10   11 10 09 08 07

Contents

The Sandy Beach Habitat

A sandy **beach** is one kind of **shoreline**. Sandy beaches are often found by the **ocean**. Many **organisms** find homes here. The sandy beach is their **habitat**. Different organisms live in different parts of the habitat. Some organisms live in the **sand**. Some live in the **beach wrack**. Some live in the **nearshore** water. Other organisms use the sandy beach but also go far beyond, into the ocean.

This book shows you what lives in the different parts of the sandy beach habitat. You will read **questions** about the organisms. The pictures may help you answer the questions. As you read, think of some questions *you* have about these organisms.

These are the parts of a sandy beach habitat. Some organisms spend time in more than one part. A herring gull can be sitting on a cliff, flying through the air, or swimming on the nearshore water. A herring gull spends most of its time on the sand, though.

The Sand

One important part of the sandy **beach habitat** is the **sand**. Many animals live in the sand. The sand keeps them safe. But the sand is always changing. Every wave moves some sand—and maybe the homes of animals! At high **tide**, water may cover the sand where these animals live.

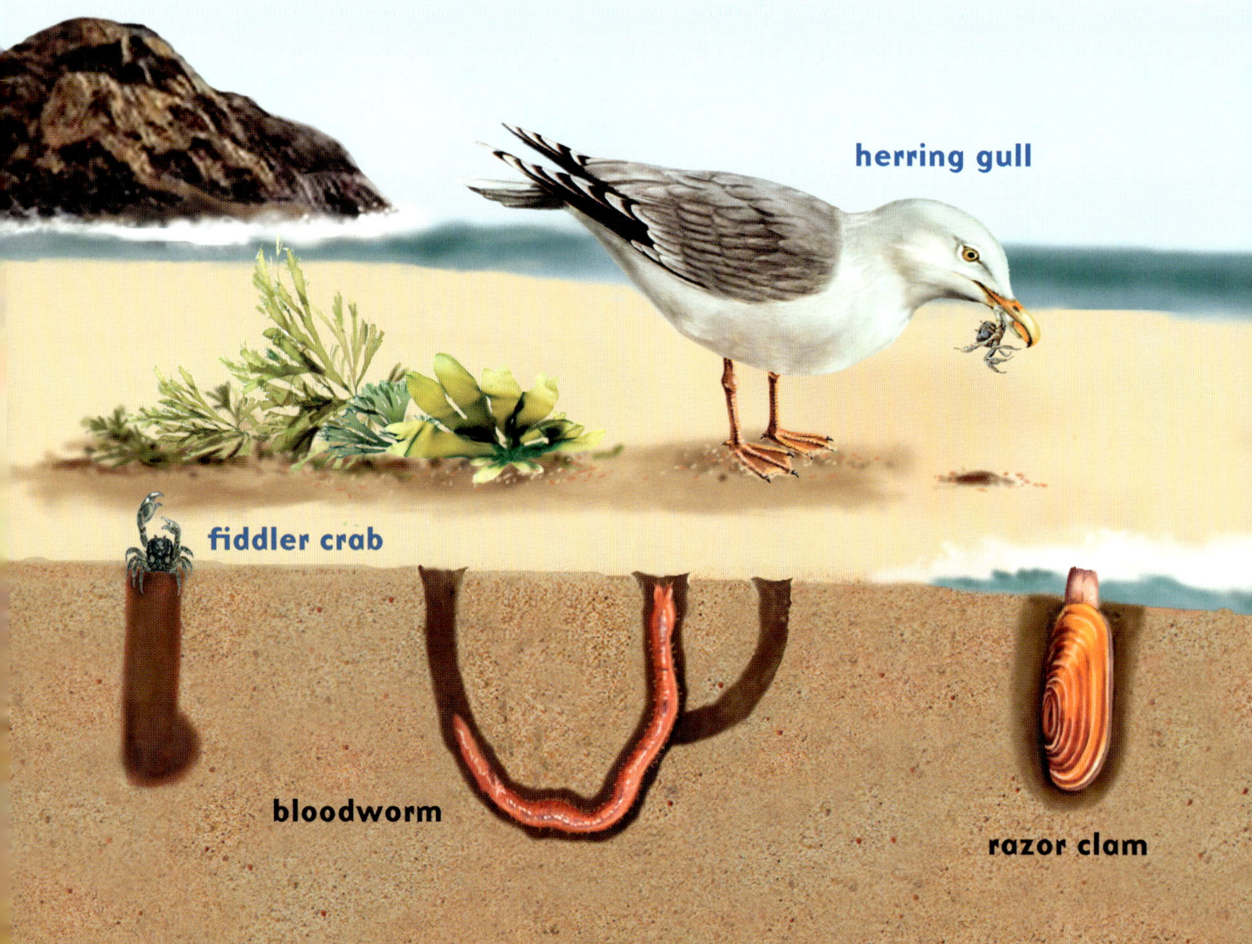

Some animals come to the beach just to eat the animals they find in the sand. Animals that catch and eat other animals are called **predators**. The animals that predators eat are called **prey**. Many birds are sandy beach predators. Crabs and clams are some of their prey.

Bloodworms

Bloodworms hide in the **sand** and wait. What do you think the bloodworms are waiting for?

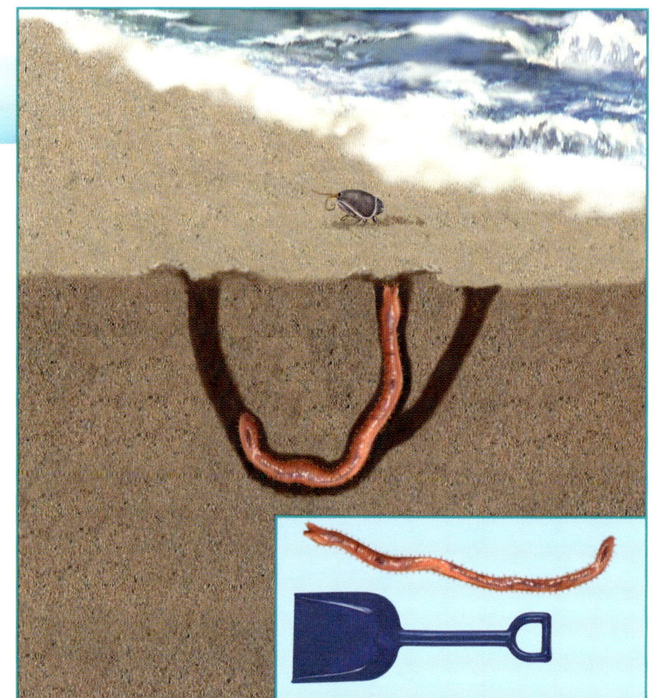

Fiddler crabs

Male fiddler crabs have one big claw and one small claw. They use the small claw to eat. What do the fiddler crabs do with the big claw?

Herring gulls

Herring gulls are not picky about their food. They will eat almost anything. What do herring gulls find to eat at the sandy **beach**?

Moon snails

Moon snails have a huge foot. A moon snail's shell looks too small, but the snail can still fit its whole foot inside! Why do you think a moon snail might need to put its foot in its shell?

Olive snails

Olive snails move around under the **sand**. Many **predators** living at the **beach** hunt for them. How do olive snails get away from the predators trying to eat them?

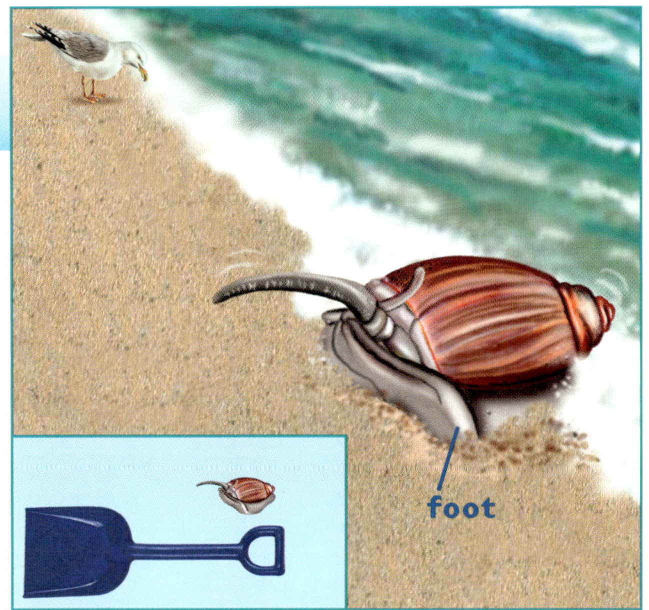

Peregrine falcons

Peregrine falcons fly high above the sandy **beach.** These birds are the fastest animals in the world. How does flying so fast help peregrine falcons **survive** at the beach?

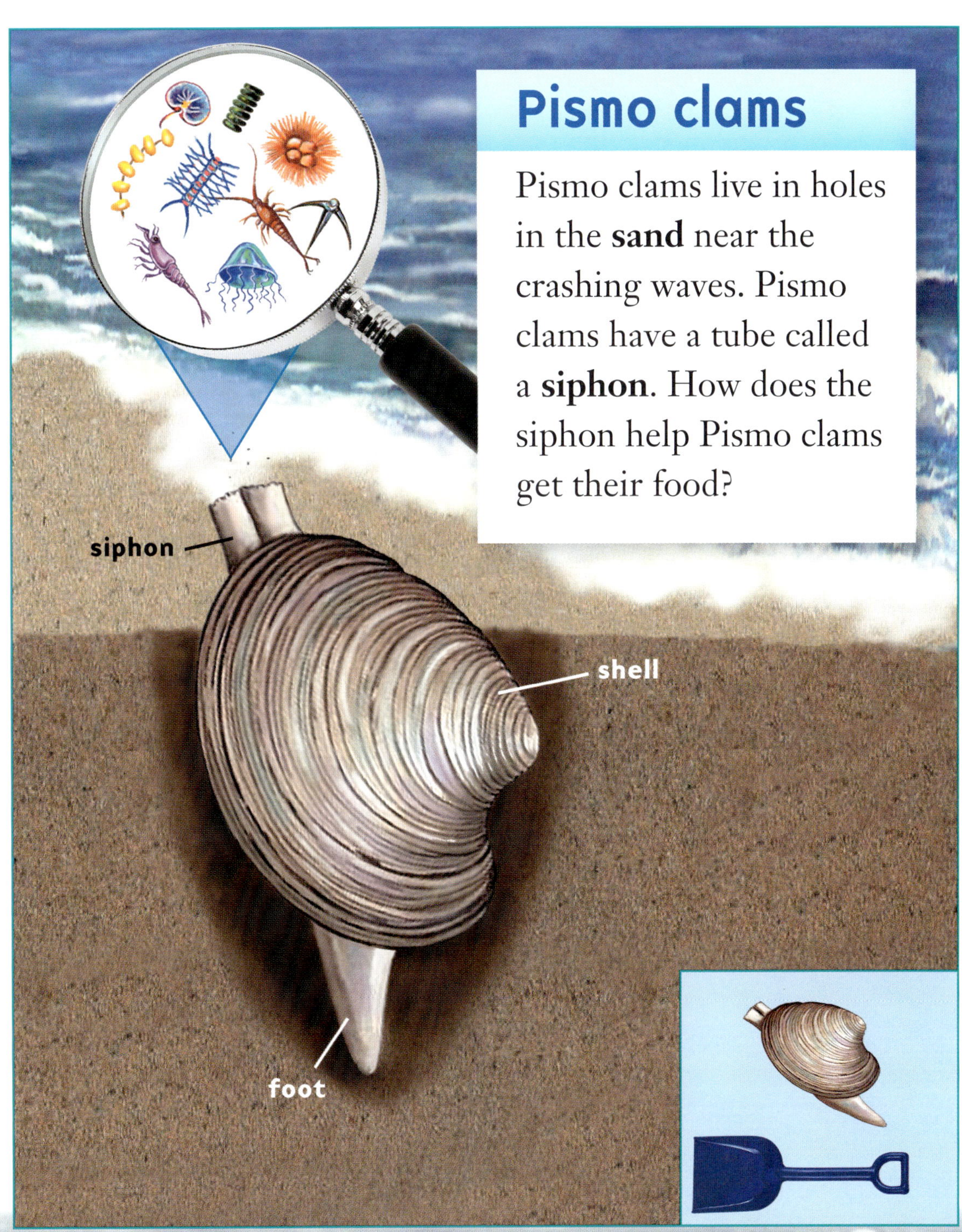

Pismo clams

Pismo clams live in holes in the **sand** near the crashing waves. Pismo clams have a tube called a **siphon**. How does the siphon help Pismo clams get their food?

Razor clams

Razor clams have thin shells. **Ocean** waves sometimes lift these clams out of their holes. Will the next wave break the razor clam's shell to pieces?

Sand crabs

Sand crabs dig holes on the **beach** near the crashing waves. The **sand** **protects** them from the waves. How do the sand crabs dig holes so fast?

Sanderlings

Sanderlings run quickly on the **shoreline**. These little birds run to the water. Then they turn and run away from the waves. They run so fast that their legs are hard to see. What are the sanderlings doing so close to the waves?

The Beach Wrack

A sandy **beach** can have **beach wrack**. Beach wrack is piles of **seaweed**, shells, dead animals, and trash. These things are brought to the beach by waves and wind. Beach wrack becomes a home for many animals. But they cannot live in one pile of wrack for long. Their home may be carried away by the next high **tide**!

kelp flies
pseudoscorpion
rove beetle
beach hopper

Beach hoppers

Beach hoppers can really jump! They have legs like springs. How do strong legs help beach hoppers live in the **beach wrack**?

Kelp flies

Kelp flies eat the **beach wrack** and lay their eggs in it, too. What makes beach wrack a good place for kelp flies to live?

Pseudoscorpions

Pseudoscorpions are tiny **predators**. They grab their **prey** with stinging claws. What kind of prey do pseudoscorpions catch with their claws?

Rove beetles

Rove beetles are **predators**. They hunt for their **prey** in the **beach wrack**. Rove beetles are prey, too. What animal is hunting for the rove beetles?

The Sandy Beach and Beyond

Some animals need the **beach** *and* the **ocean**. These animals spend most of their lives swimming in the ocean. But without the beach, they would not **survive**. The beach is where they have their babies or lay their eggs. Some of these animals also use the beach as a place to rest and get away from **marine predators**.

harbor seals

elephant seals
loggerhead
sea turtle

Elephant seals

Elephant seals are the biggest of all seals. They eat and even sleep in the water. All seals are great swimmers, but they cannot move very well on land. Why are these elephant seals on the **beach**?

Harbor seals

Harbor seals spend a lot of time in the water. They cannot walk on their **flippers** at all. How do harbor seals move on the **beach**?

Leatherback sea turtles

Leatherback sea turtles are fast swimmers. They find their food out in the **ocean** far from **shore**. Why do leatherback sea turtles come to the **beach**?

Loggerhead sea turtles

Loggerhead sea turtles have a huge head and powerful jaws. What do these **predators** find to eat at the **shoreline**?

The Nearshore Water

Many **organisms** live in the **nearshore** water. Nearshore water is the water close to the **shore**. This is the water where people swim. Some of the organisms here are swimmers, too. Some organisms drift in the waves and **currents**. Some organisms dig in the **sand** under the water. The nearshore organisms cannot **survive** out of the water.

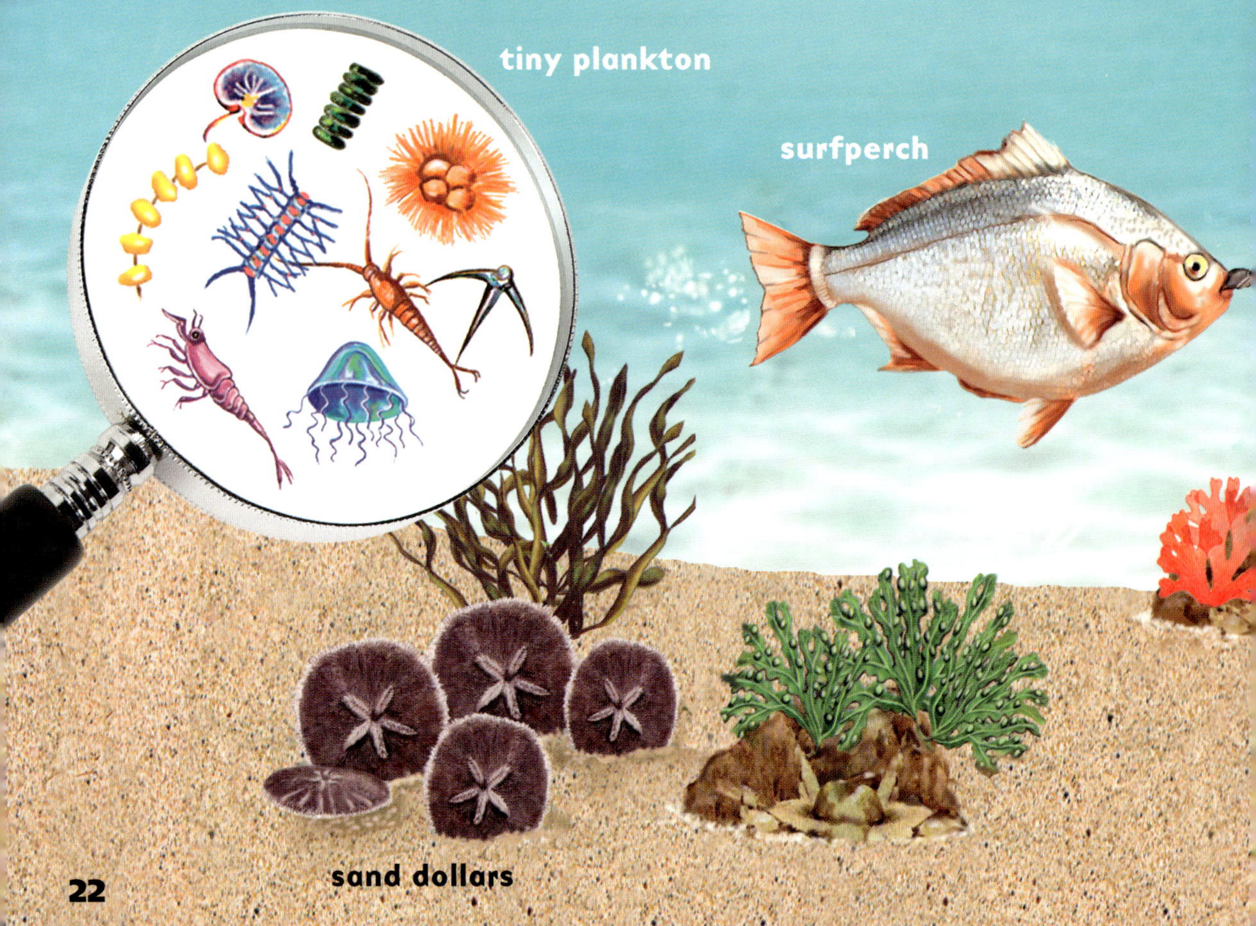

jellyfish
striped mullet
armored sea star

Armored sea stars

Armored sea stars move very fast over the **sand** under the water. They are hunting for **prey**. How do armored sea stars catch their prey?

Jellyfish

Jellyfish are not strong swimmers. They drift along in the **ocean**. How do jellyfish catch fish to eat?

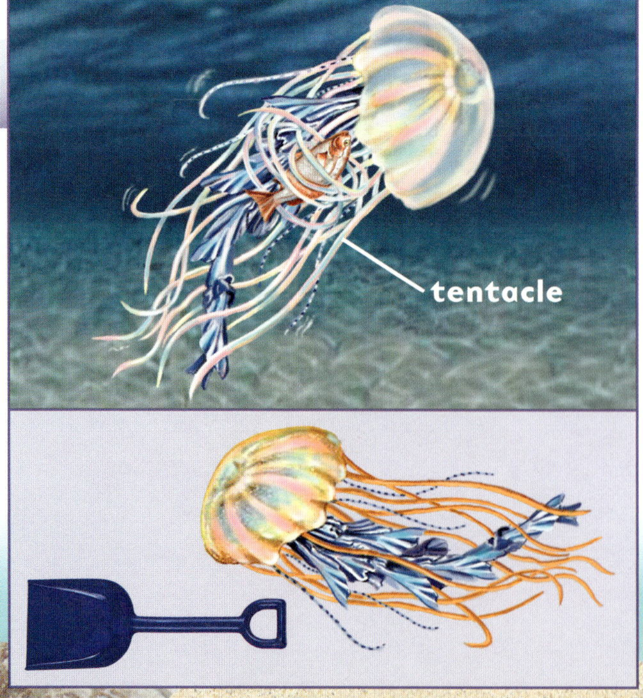

Sand dollars

Many people have never seen a living sand dollar. Dead sand dollars on the **beach** look smooth and white. Do you notice anything surprising about living sand dollars?

Striped mullets

Striped mullets can jump high out of the **ocean**. Then they crash back into the water. Why do striped mullets jump so high out of the water?

Surfperch

Surfperch swim in the **ocean** near where the waves crash. What are the surfperch doing so close to the **beach**?

Tiny plankton

These little animals and plants drift in the **ocean**. Tiny plankton are hard to see because they are so small. What animals eat tiny plankton?

Glossary

beach: a place along the shore of a lake, river, or ocean that is covered with loose material like sand, pebbles, or mud

beach wrack: piles of seaweed and other things carried to the beach by waves and wind

current: the flow of water through the ocean or a river

flipper: a wide, flat, leg-like body part used for swimming

habitat: where an organism lives and gets everything it needs to survive

marine: having to do with the ocean

nearshore: the part of the ocean that is close to the shore

ocean: the salt water that covers most of the Earth

organism: a living thing such as a plant or an animal

predator: an animal that hunts and eats other animals

prey: an animal that is hunted and eaten by other animals

protect: to keep someone or something safe

question: something someone wonders or asks about

sand: small, broken-up pieces of different materials, such as shells and rocks

seaweed: a plant-like living thing that grows in the ocean

shore: the land along the edge of water

shoreline: the place where water meets the land

siphon: a body part shaped like a long tube, used to suck in water and tiny plankton

survive: to stay alive

tide: the daily changes in the ocean's water level that can usually be observed at the shoreline

Index

Page numbers in **bold** show an organism's main page.